ADVANCED
PRESENTATIONS

ABOUT THIS BOOK

Advanced Presentations is an easy-to-follow guide to using some of the more sophisticated features of Microsoft's PowerPoint 2000 program to create dynamic presentations.

OWERPOINT 2000 IS AN EXTREMELY versatile piece of software that allows users to create their own multimedia presentations, add and edit text, images, sounds, animations as well as charts and tables. To get the best from this book, some knowledge of the program will be useful: although complete novices will still be able to work through the features shown, they might find it useful to first read and use the accompanying volume *Creating Presentations*, which deals with the program's basic features.

Advanced Presentations takes a step-by-step approach to mastering the advanced features of the program. Each step is accompanied by an illustration showing you exactly how your own screen should look when you follow the instructions correctly. The first chapter explains the various toolbars in detail. It is worth studying these, as mastery of the toolbars is crucial to the efficient use of PowerPoint 2000, avoiding the need to use the more time-consuming drop-down menus.

The book contains several features to help you understand both what is happening and what you need to do.

Command keys, such as ENTER and CTRL, are shown in these rectangles: Enter ↵ and Ctrl, so that there's no confusion, for example, over whether you should press that key or type the letters "ctrl."

Cross-references are shown in the text as left- or right-hand page icons: ⬑ and ⬐. The page number and the reference are shown at the foot of the page.

As well as the step-by-step sections, there are boxes that explain certain features in detail, and tip boxes that provide you with alternative methods. Finally, at the back, you will find a glossary of common terms and a comprehensive index.

ESSENTIAL **DK** COMPUTERS

MULTIMEDIA

ADVANCED PRESENTATIONS

TERRY BURROWS

A Dorling Kindersley Book

Dorling Kindersley
LONDON, NEW YORK, SYDNEY, DELHI,
PARIS, MUNICH, and JOHANNESBURG

Produced for Dorling Kindersley Limited by
Design Revolution, Queens Park Villa,
30 West Drive, Brighton, East Sussex BN2 2GE

EDITORIAL DIRECTOR Ian Whitelaw
SENIOR DESIGNER Andy Ashdown
PROJECT EDITOR John Watson
DESIGNERS Andrew Easton and Paul Bowler

SENIOR EDITOR Mary Lindsay
SENIOR MANAGING ART EDITOR Nigel Duffield
DTP DESIGNER Jason Little
PRODUCTION CONTROLLER Wendy Penn

Published in Great Britain in 2000 by
Dorling Kindersley Limited,
9 Henrietta Street, London WC2E 8PS

2 4 6 8 10 9 7 5 3 1

A CIP catalog record for this book is available from the British Library.

ISBN 0-7513-2900-2

Color reproduced by First Impressions, London
Printed in Italy by Graphicom

See our complete
catalog at
www.dk.com

CONTENTS

STARTING POWERPOINT

Although PowerPoint 2000 is recognizable from its appearance
as a part of the Office 2000 suite of programs, it uniquely
blends multimedia features into a powerful presentation tool.

WHAT IS POWERPOINT 2000?

At some point, most of us have to give a presentation. This could mean telling a group of friends how to get from one location to another, or it could be a president of a corporation talking to the shareholders. However, in both situations the basic aim is to convey information.

Although it is possible to stand and read from a script, it's far easier to retain interest and consolidate the message by using visual cues. For an effective presentation, the speaker must back up the script with overhead projections, slides, handouts, and speaker's notes.

WHAT IS A POWERPOINT PRESENTATION?

Imagine a computer program that can structure and create dynamic visual presentations, which include full-color images, sounds, animations, charts, and graphs. Imagine, too, that it enables you to prepare handouts to accompany each slide in your presentation. Finally, imagine that you could run the presentation on your computer. Microsoft PowerPoint 2000 is capable of all this and more.

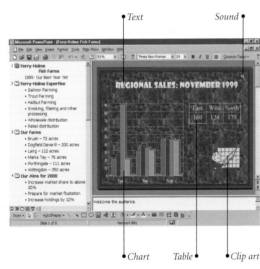

● *Text*   *Sound* ●

● *Chart*   *Table* ●   ● *Clip art*

LAUNCHING POWERPOINT

To run PowerPoint 2000, switch on your PC and go into Windows – in most cases this should happen automatically.

Microsoft PowerPoint 2000 will work happily with Windows 95, Windows 98, and Windows NT.

THE POWERPOINT DIALOG BOX

● Click on the **Start** button on the Task bar.

● From the pop-up menu, point to **Program**.

● From the drop-down menu, click on **Microsoft PowerPoint**.

● If you can't find PowerPoint in the **Program** folder, then it probably has not been installed on your PC. PowerPoint 2000 is generally supplied as a part of the Microsoft Office 2000 suite of programs. If you have a problem, go back to the original CDs – or, better still, get someone more experienced to do it for you.

● Each time you launch PowerPoint 2000, the first screen that you meet is a **PowerPoint** dialog box. This provides you with four options before you finally get to see the main **PowerPoint** window. Click on **OK**.

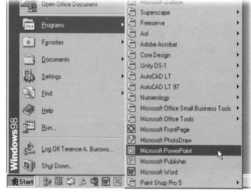

THE POWERPOINT WINDOW

The main body of the window is split into two segments. On the left-hand side you are given an overview of the structure and content of the different slides that make up your presentation. The screen on the right shows the currently active slide. This is the screen in which you can edit and add to the contents of the slide.

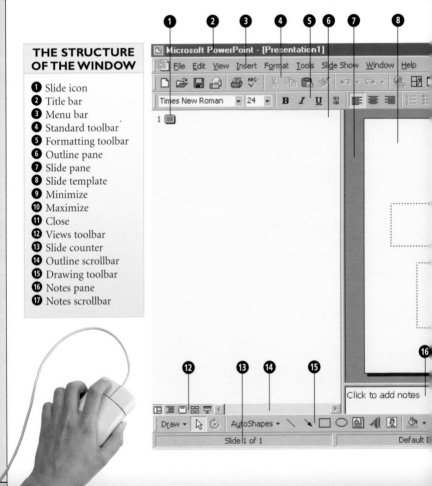

THE STRUCTURE OF THE WINDOW

1. Slide icon
2. Title bar
3. Menu bar
4. Standard toolbar
5. Formatting toolbar
6. Outline pane
7. Slide pane
8. Slide template
9. Minimize
10. Maximize
11. Close
12. Views toolbar
13. Slide counter
14. Outline scrollbar
15. Drawing toolbar
16. Notes pane
17. Notes scrollbar

MOVING THE TOOLBARS

If the Formatting toolbar does not appear below the Standard toolbar, place the cursor over the Formatting toolbar "handle." When the four-headed arrow appears (right), hold down the mouse button and drag the toolbar into position.

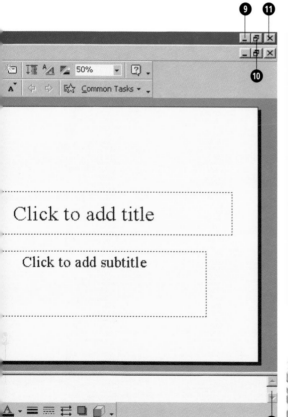

Click to add title

Click to add subtitle

Toolbar layout options

You are not limited to having the toolbars positioned along the top of the screen – it's possible to place them anywhere on the main window. A commonly used alternative is to drag the toolbars to either side of the screen where they appear as vertical bars. You can either click on the toolbar handle or on an inactive part of the toolbar and drag it to your preferred location.

THE POWERPOINT TOOLBARS

The icons below the Title bar are grouped into toolbars. When PowerPoint 2000 is first installed, the two main toolbars – Standard and Formatting – occupy a single row 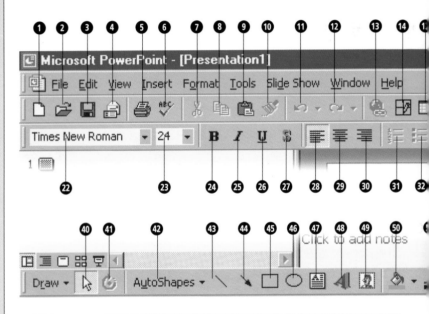; one is shown below the other here for clarity. At the foot of the window when you first run PowerPoint 2000, the Drawing toolbar appears, which contains the common graphics commands that can be applied to your presentations.

THE FORMATTING TOOLBAR

㉒ Font	㉘ Align left	㉞ Decrease font size
㉓ Font size	㉙ Center	㉟ Promote
㉔ Bold	㉚ Align right	㊱ Demote
㉕ Italic	㉛ Numbered list	㊲ Animation effects
㉖ Underline	㉜ Bulleted list	㊳ Common tasks menu
㉗ Shadow	㉝ Increase font size	㊴ More buttons

9 Moving the toolbars

THE STANDARD TOOLBAR

1. New
2. Open
3. Save
4. Email
5. Print
6. Spelling
7. Cut
8. Copy
9. Paste
10. Format painter
11. Undo
12. Redo
13. Insert hyperlink
14. Tables and borders
15. Insert table
16. Insert chart
17. New slide
18. Expand all
19. Show formatting
20. Grayscale preview
21. Zoom

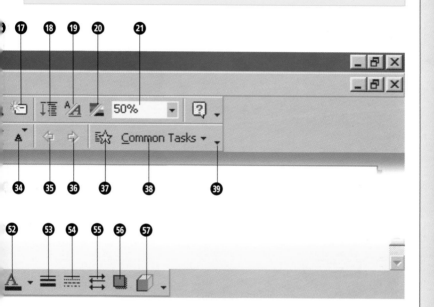

THE DRAWING TOOLBAR

40. Select objects
41. Free rotate
42. AutoShapes menu
43. Line
44. Arrow
45. Rectangle
46. Oval
47. Text box
48. Insert WordArt
49. Insert Clip Art
50. Fill color
51. Line color
52. Font color
53. Line style
54. Dash style
55. Arrow style
56. Shadow
57. 3-D

POWERPOINT SHORTCUTS

PowerPoint 2000 contains a great many shortcuts that can help you to conduct your presentations more smoothly and efficiently. The most effective of these are keyboard shortcuts that enable users to perform commands by pressing keys rather than selecting options from the drop-down menus.

A USEFUL SELECTION

By pressing Ctrl *+B you can quickly change selected text to bold.*

The key combination of Ctrl *+W closes your presentation.*

Select all objects (in Slide view)	Ctrl +A
Select all text (in Outline view)	Ctrl +A
Select all slides (in Slider Sorter view)	Ctrl +A
Bold	Ctrl +B
Copy	Ctrl +C
Duplicate	Ctrl +D
Center alignment	Ctrl +E
Find	Ctrl +F
Turn guides on or off	Ctrl +G
Replace	Ctrl +H
Italicize	Ctrl +I
Justify text	Ctrl +J
Insert hyperlink	Ctrl +K
Align to left	Ctrl +L
Insert new slide	Ctrl +M
Start new presentation	Ctrl +N
Open a presentation	Ctrl +O
Print a presentation	Ctrl +P
Exit PowerPoint 2000	Ctrl +Q
Align to right	Ctrl +R
Save presentation	Ctrl +S
Format font	Ctrl +T
Underline text	Ctrl +U
Paste	Ctrl +V
Close presentation	Ctrl +W
Cut	Ctrl +X
Repeat last command or action	Ctrl +Y
Undo last command or action	Ctrl +Z

SHORTCUTS USING FUNCTION KEYS

Help F1
Toggle between selecting all text within an object or the object itself. F2
Run presentation F5
Spelling F7

HOTKEYS WHEN RUNNING A SLIDE SHOW

Advance to the next slide . . . . $\boxed{\rightarrow}$
   " . . . . Left mouse click
   " . . . . $\boxed{\text{Spacebar}}$
   " . . . . N
   " . . . . $\boxed{\downarrow}$
   " . . . . $\boxed{\text{Enter} \leftarrow}$
   " . . . . $\boxed{\text{PgDn}}$
Return to previous slide . . . . $\boxed{\leftarrow}$
   " . . . . $\boxed{\leftarrow \text{Bksp}}$
   " . . . . P
   " . . . . $\boxed{\uparrow}$
   " . . . . $\boxed{\text{PgUp}}$
Advance to slide with any given number . . . . Any number followed by $\boxed{\text{Enter} \leftarrow}$
Blackout screen on/off . . . . B or . [period]
Whiteout screen on/off . . . . W or , [comma]
Arrow pointer on/off . . . . A or =
Automatic slide show start/stop . . . . S or +
End presentation . . . . $\boxed{\text{Ctrl}} + \boxed{\text{Break}}$
   " . . . . $\boxed{\text{Esc}}$
   " . . . . - [hyphen]
Erase drawing on screen . . . . E
Go to hidden slide . . . . H
Rehearse using new times . . . . T
Rehearse using original times . . . . O
Rehearse using mouse click to advance . . . . M
Change pointer to pen shape . . . . $\boxed{\text{Ctrl}} + P$
Change pointer to arrow shape . . . . $\boxed{\text{Ctrl}} + A$
Pointer and button show/hide . . . . $\boxed{\text{Ctrl}} + U$

When running a slide show,
$\boxed{\leftarrow \text{Bksp}}$ *will return you to*
the previous slide.

THE MASTERS

In this chapter we'll be looking at how you can exert more control over the appearance and content of your slides by using PowerPoint 2000's Master features.

THE SLIDE MASTER

The most important of these features is the Slide Master. This is a facility for controlling certain characteristics within your presentation. Having, for example, set up a presentation made up of several hundred slides, you may decide that you want to alter specific design features throughout. Instead of having to edit each slide one by one, you can use the Slide Master to alter them all at the same time.

1 OPENING THE SLIDE MASTER

● To open the **Slide Master**, choose **Master** from the **View** menu. From the submenu, choose **Slide Master**.

● Please note: All the slides illustrated in this book have been created by using a **Design Template** selected from the opening **PowerPoint** dialog box.

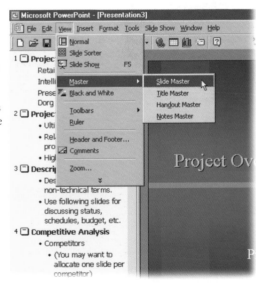

● The **Slide Master** view appears. This contains placeholders for all the basic parts of a slide you are likely to need. Any changes made on the **Slide** Master are also made on all slides. A floating **Master** toolbar also appears.

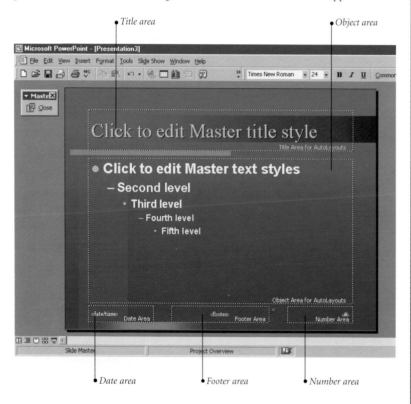

● *Title area*

● *Object area*

● *Date area*

● *Footer area*

● *Number area*

THE OBJECT AREA

On the **Slide Master**, the object area in which the bulk of the information is created has five different levels of text. Each of these levels can be given font attributes that can be set up and amended in exactly the same way as the title area. In each case, all you have to do is to click anywhere on the text line and call up the **Font** dialog box as shown on the following page.

2 CHANGING FONTS

● Any changes that you make to any of the objects are made throughout the entire presentation. In this example, we'll alter the font used on the title area.

● In the **Slide Master** view, click anywhere on the title area.

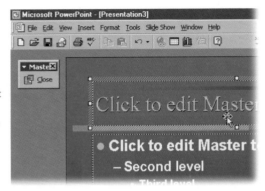

● Click on **Format** in the Menu bar and select **Font**.

● Enter the new font specifications in the **Font** dialog box and click on **OK**.

Font selector ●

Font style selector ●

Size selector ●

● The new title area font is
displayed in the **Slide
Master** view.

● To see how this has
affected your presentation,
leave the **Slide Master** view
by clicking on **Close** in the
floating **Master** toolbar.

● As you can see, the font
has been changed on all the
slides based on the **Slide
Master**.

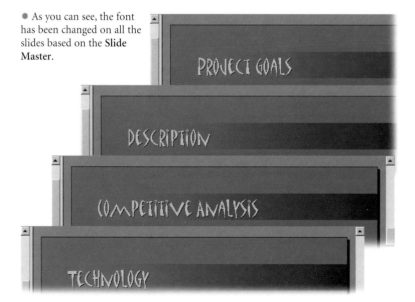

HEADERS AND FOOTERS

In the **Slide Master** view there are other object boxes at the foot of the slide: the date area, the footer area, and the number area. These can be used to hold additional information, which again, will be shown on every slide (except the title slide 📄). These attributes can be set up using the **Header And Footer** dialog box.

1 SETTING UP THE SLIDE NUMBER

● To set up a slide number for inclusion on each slide, open the **Slide Master** view 📄 and choose **Header and Footer** from the drop-down **View** menu.

● The **Header and Footer** dialog box opens. Click on the **Slide** tab if it is not already at the front.
● Click in the **Slide number** check box, and then click on the **Apply to All** button. The **Header and Footer** dialog box closes.

The Slide number check box ●

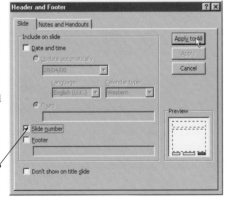

	The Title		The Slide
23	Master	14	Master

● The **Slide Master** view
will not have obviously
changed, but if you look at
a slide in your presentation,
you will see the number
displayed in the right-hand
corner of the slide.

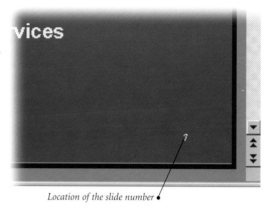

Location of the slide number ●

2 ADDING TEXT TO A SLIDE NUMBER

● You can customize the
slide number by returning
to the **Slide Master** view.
The set of symbols: <#> in
the number area indicates
that a slide number is to be
inserted.

● Click immediately before
these symbols and the
cursor becomes an
insertion point allowing
you to add text. You might
want, for example, to insert
the word **SLIDE**.

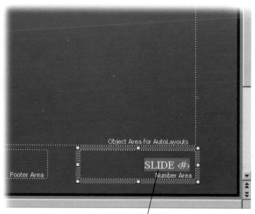

Text added to slide number ●

ZOOMING IN

The default size of the
text in the header and
footer areas is very small.
You may find it much
easier to edit this information by resizing the screen.
To do this, choose **Zoom**
from the **View** menu. The
Zoom dialog box usually
defaults to **Fit**. By selecting
a zoom value of **100%** or
more, you can position
the cursor more easily
and see what is happening
in the larger display.

● Font attributes of slide-number text can be changed as you can with other text ⬚. Highlight the text, and make your choices in the **Font** dialog box after selecting **Font** from the Format toolbar.

● If you now leave the **Slide Master** view you will see that each slide (except the title slide) has its number displayed, and the number is prefixed by the word **SLIDE**.

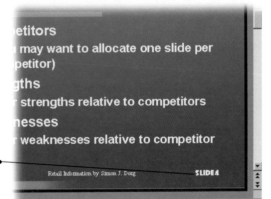

The newly formatted number area style

3 ADDING FOOTER TEXT

● The footer area allows you to display the same piece of text on every slide. A typical example would be a company name or the overall title of the presentation.

● In the **Slide Master** view, choose **Header and Footer** from the **View** menu.

● In the **Header and Footer** dialog box, click on the **Slide** tab. Click in the **Footer** check box and then type into the text box the text that you want to be displayed on each slide.

● When you have finished, click on the **Apply to all** button.

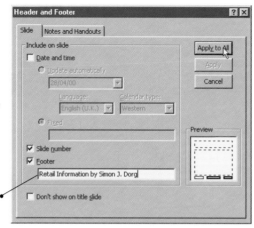

Footer text box

● Once again, the **Slide Master** view appears unchanged, but if you look at your presentation you will see that the text appears on every slide.

Footer text in the slide

4 DELETING AND MOVING OBJECTS

● It is possible to delete or move header and footer objects.

● In the **Slide Master** view, the date area on the bottom left-hand corner has not been used, and can be deleted. To do this, simply click on the object and press the [Del] key.

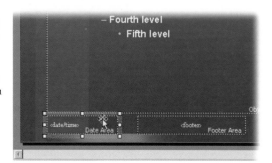

● You can now move the footer area to the left-hand edge of the slide. Click on the object, hold down the mouse button, and drag and drop the object into the new position.

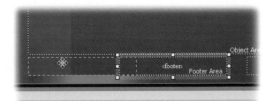

● The fact that the text marked <**footer**> is in the center of the box indicates that it has been center-aligned. As the footer area is now on the left-hand edge of the slide, the appearance would be improved if the text were to be aligned with the left-hand edge.

● Highlight the footer area and choose **Alignment** from the **Format** menu. Choose **Align Left** from the submenu.

● If you look at the Slide Show view you will now see that the footer text is aligned down the left-hand edge on each slide except the title slide.

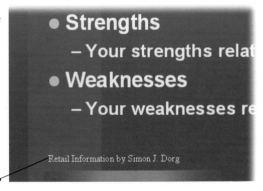

Left-aligned footer ●

THE OTHER MASTERS

There are three other Master features – **Title Master**, **Handout Master**, and **Notes Master**. Although they are not used as frequently as the **Slide Master**, they each have their own specific functions to help in the development of presentations.

THE TITLE MASTER

The **Title Master** can be used in much the same way as the **Slide Master**, except that the changes made will only affect title slides. If you look at the title slide for the presentation you have just been working on, you will see that although the *settings* created in the **Header and Footer** dialog box also appear in the title slide, the *amendments* made in the **Slide Master** do not. We can alter these aspects in the **Title Master** view.

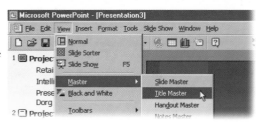

1 THE TITLE MASTER VIEW

● Choose **Master** from the **View** menu, and select **Title Master** from the submenu.
● The **Title Master** view appears. You can edit this in the same way as the **Slide Master** view.

● In this example, we will delete the following areas: the **Date Area**, **Footer Area**, and **Number Area** because these are not relevant components of the title slide. In each case, click on the object to select it, and then press the Del key.

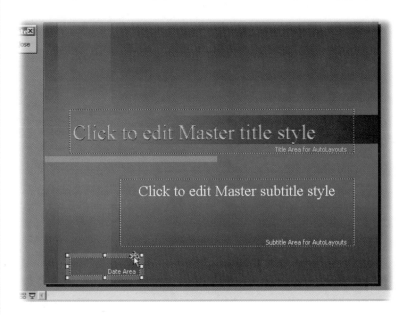

● Now click on the **Normal view** button in the Views toolbar ⬛.

● You can see that the footer and slide number information no longer appear on the title slide.

Retail Information
Intelligent Systems PLC
Presented by Simon J. Dorg

8 ⓬ **Views toolbar**

● Take a look at slide 2. You can see that your alterations to the title slide have not affected the others.

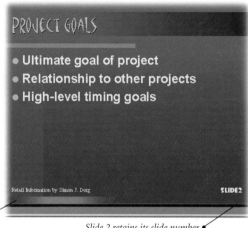

The footer is still present on slide 2

Slide 2 retains its slide number

2 THE HANDOUT MASTER

● As you probably know, PowerPoint 2000 allows you to prepare hard-copy handouts from your slide presentation. These are essentially smaller, printed versions of the slides. The **Handout Master** allows you to alter the format of your handouts and to add further details, such as the company name and logo.

● Choose **Master** from the **View** menu, and select **Handout Master** from the submenu.

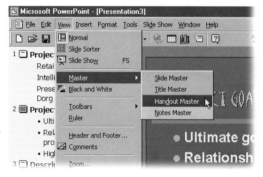

NO TITLE MASTER OPTION?

If your presentation does not have a title slide, or if you are working with a blank presentation that has no design template applied to it, you will not be able to use the **Title Master**. In these cases, this option will appear grayed-out in the menu.

● The **Handout Master** view and the **Handout Master** toolbar both appear. From here, you can select the number of slides that appear on each page and edit the header, date, footer, and number in the area allocated to each.

*The **Handout Master** toolbar*

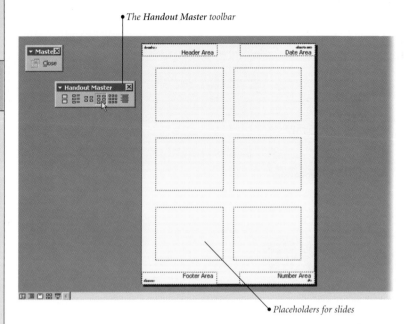

Placeholders for slides

● The **Header Area**, **Date Area**, **Footer Area**, and **Number Area** placeholders can all be edited, resized, moved, or deleted in the same way as with the **Slide** and **Title Master** screens. If you delete these placeholders they can be recalled using the **Handout Master Layout** dialog box.
● Choose **Handout Master Layout** from the **Format** menu.

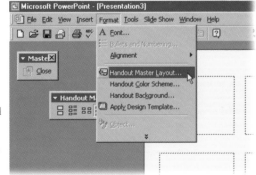

● The **Handout Master Layout** dialog box appears. Click in the placeholders that you want to be included and click on **OK**.
● The selected placeholder areas are reinstated in the **Handout Master** view.

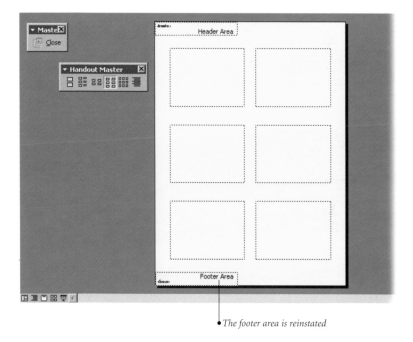

• *The footer area is reinstated*

NOTES MASTER

Each slide can be set up to include a notes page to contain an accompanying script. Each page contains a picture of the slide with your notes printed out beneath. The **Notes Master** view allows you to edit the information on this page. You use the same place- holders as in the **Handout Master** and alter the space allocated to the slide on the page, making more room for the text.

ADVANCED DESIGN

PowerPoint 2000's more advanced design features include the use of images either from PowerPoint's own ClipArt gallery or from your own image files.

INTRODUCING CLIPART

The PowerPoint 2000 package includes a large gallery of ClipArt containing images that can be used to enhance and emphasize your presentations. Once you have inserted an image, PowerPoint contains features to manipulate the image.

1 INSERTING A CLIPART IMAGE
● Begin by selecting the slide on which you want a picture inserted. Choose **Picture** from the **Insert** menu, and from the submenu select **ClipArt**.

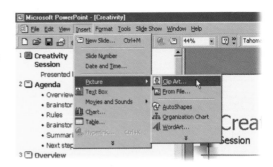

2 SELECTING PHOTOGRAPHS
● The **Insert ClipArt** dialog box appears. Scroll down through the categories and click on the **Photographs** option.

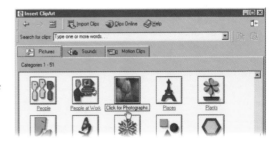

3 PREVIEWING THE IMAGE

● Click on any image and a pop-up toolbar will appear. Click on the **Preview clip** button to see an enlarged version of the picture. The same button can be used to close the preview.

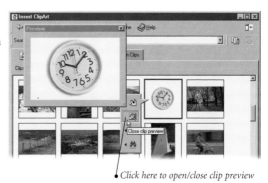

Click here to open/close clip preview

4 INSERTING THE IMAGE

● Click on the **Insert clip** button on the pop-up toolbar to place the photograph on the slide.

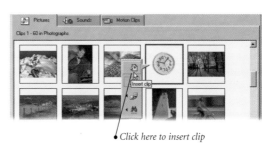

Click here to insert clip

5 THE SLIDE WITH THE IMAGE

● Click on the **Close** button of the **Insert ClipArt** dialog box, and you will see that the picture is now positioned in the center of the slide. This is the default position for all objects loaded from the clip gallery.

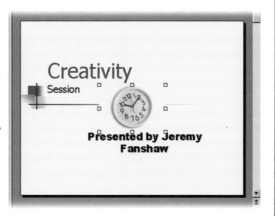

REPOSITIONING CLIPART

There will be occasions when you want the ClipArt image placed in the center of your slide, but more often you will want to move it. The image can easily be moved, and you can also resize it to fit the location where you want it to be placed.

MOVING THE IMAGE

● Click once to select the object, which is then surrounded by eight resizing handles.

● Hold down the left mouse button and move the object by using the drag-and-drop technique. While you are dragging the object, an outline box indicates its new, current position.

● Release the mouse button when the image is in place.

USING THE ARROW KEYS

You can also use the four arrow keys on the keyboard to move selected objects. These are especially useful for precise positioning. For very fine movements, hold down the [Ctrl] key while moving the object with the arrow keys.

RESIZING CLIPART

It is unlikely that the default size of the ClipArt image will meet the needs of your presentation slide. However, PowerPoint 2000 makes it easy to proportionally alter the dimensions of an image simply by dragging one of the four corner handles.

1 PROPORTIONAL RESIZING

● When a picture is selected, you will notice that the mouse pointer changes its icon to a double-headed arrow when placed over the handles that surround the object. By dragging and releasing these handles, you can rescale the picture.

● Drag and release one of the corner handles to resize the object while retaining its proportions.

2 STRETCHING AND COMPRESSING

● When the mouse pointer passes over one of the side handles, the pointer again changes to a double-headed arrow. Dragging one of the side handles allows you to stretch or compress the image in the chosen direction.

● Place the mouse cursor over one of the side handles, hold down the left mouse button and the cursor changes to a cross hair. An outline of the image follows the cursor.

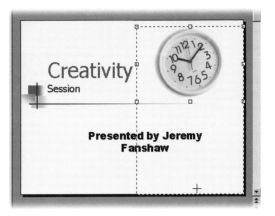

● Release the mouse button when the image is the required shape.

STACKING OBJECTS

As you can see, the elongated piece of ClipArt has now covered some of the text. You will very rarely want this to happen, and PowerPoint contains a feature to deal with this. Any number of objects can be layered, or "stacked," on top of each other.

By default, PowerPoint stacks objects in the order in which they were created, with the most recently created object occupying the uppermost layer. This sequence can be altered by using the **Order** command in the Drawing toolbar .

1 SELECTING THE OBJECT

● In this example, we want to place the original text on the top layer. Click anywhere within the object that you intend to reorder, so that it is highlighted.

2 REORDERING THE OBJECT

● Click on **Draw** in the Drawing toolbar. From the pop-up menu select **Order**. On the submenu click on **Bring to Front**.

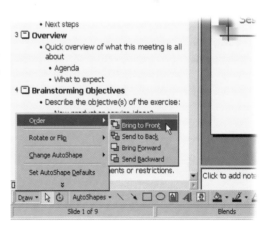

⑮ Drawing toolbar

8

3 DESELECTING THE OBJECT

● When you deselect the text box (by clicking off the box – anywhere else on the slide), the text appears superimposed on top of the image.

SELECTING FROM SEVERAL OBJECTS

In certain circumstances, your slide may contain several objects that are layered one above the other. This may make it difficult to select the object that you want to reorder. PowerPoint 2000 has an easy solution to this problem. Click on any one of the layered objects and then press the [Tab⇆] key repeatedly until the object that you want to reorder becomes highlighted.

INSERTING YOUR OWN PICTURES

Although the ClipArt gallery contains a large selection of images for you to insert into your presentations, in many cases you will want to use your own pictures from files stored on your hard disk. PowerPoint makes this a very simple process.

1 SELECTING THE FILE OPTION

● Begin by selecting the slide that you want to illustrate. Choose **Picture** from the **Insert** menu, and from the submenu that appears click on **From File**.

2 SELECTING THE PICTURE

● The **Insert Picture** dialog box opens. Use either the **Look in:** feature or the files in the central panel of the dialog box to find the picture you want. Click on the file name and a preview appears on the right-hand panel. Click on **Insert** to place the image in the slide.

3 ALTERING THE ATTRIBUTES

● You can alter attributes of the picture by using the Picture toolbar. To display the toolbar, choose **Toolbars** from the **View** menu. From the submenu, click on **Picture**.

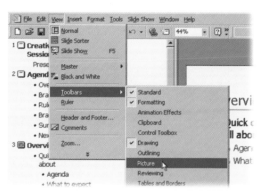

THE PICTURE TOOLBAR

The Picture toolbar contains a variety of tools for manipulating images.

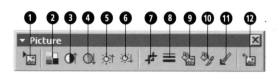

THE PICTURE TOOLBAR

❶ Insert image	❺ More brightness	❾ Recolor picture
❷ Image control	❻ Less brightness	❿ Format picture
❸ More contrast	❼ Crop	⓫ Set transparent color
❹ Less contrast	❽ Line style	⓬ Reset picture

CROPPING THE PICTURE

When you insert an image contained in a file on your hard disk, the full-size image appears in the slide. If you want to display only part of the image, you can select a specific area of the image to be included by using the **Crop** command.

1 SELECTING THE CROP COMMAND
● Click on the picture so that it is highlighted. Choose the **Crop** command on the Picture toolbar.

Crop tool ●

2 DRAGGING A FRAME HANDLE
● When the mouse pointer is placed over one of the eight handles around the image, the icon changes. Drag a handle in the same way as when resizing a picture ▢. This time the scale of the picture remains unaltered – only the frame is affected.

Handle being dragged by the crop tool ●

31 **Resizing ClipArt**

● When you deselect the picture, you can see that right-hand edge of the frame has been reduced without altering the scale of the picture. In the example shown, all four sides have been altered.

EDITING THE IMAGE

In the same way that you might want to alter the size of an image, you can also change its appearance by using the **Contrast** and **Brightness** buttons on the Picture toolbar. Each click on any of these changes the image a certain amount.

1 THE MORE CONTRAST TOOL
● To increase the contrast of your image, select the image and choose the **More Contrast** tool from the Picture toolbar.

2 THE LESS CONTRAST TOOL
● To reduce the contrast, use the **Less Contrast** tool on the same toolbar.

3 USING THE TOOLS

● Each time you use either of these commands, the contrast will be altered a little more. These two before-and-after shots illustrate the effect of increasing the contrast.

Unaltered ●

Contrast increased ten times (10 clicks on the More Contrast tool) ●

4 THE BRIGHTNESS TOOLS

● We can show the same effect for the **Brightness** tools. To increase the brightness for your image, choose the **More Brightness** button from the Picture toolbar.

● To reduce the brightness, use the **Less Brightness** tool on the same toolbar.

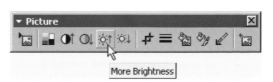

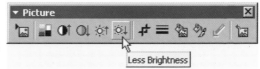

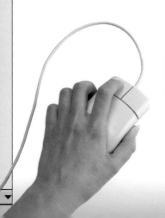

Unaltered ●

Brightness decreased ten times (10 clicks on the Less Brightness tool) ●

IMAGE CONTROL

The Image Control command provides four options: **Automatic** returns the picture to its default color; **Grayscale** uses shades of gray; **Black & White** creates a monochrome image; and **Watermark** creates a faded effect for a background.

1 SELECTING AN OPTION
● Click on the **Image Control** button ▢ on the Picture toolbar, and select one of the four options.

The Image Control button •

● The four different effects are shown here.

Using a Watermark
You may want to have a watermark image visible on all your slides – for example, you may wish your company logo to be on every one. To do this, simply open the Slide Master ▢, insert the image, and use the **Image control** to turn it into a watermark. To place it on the title slide (as well as, or instead of, all the other slides), follow these steps on the Title Master ▢.

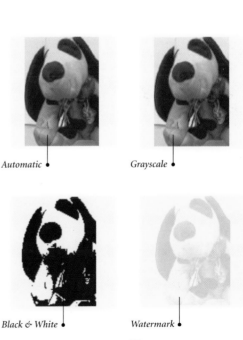

Automatic •   *Grayscale* •

Black & White •   *Watermark* •

| 35 | ❷ Image control | 14 | Opening the slide master | 23 | The title master |

CREATING YOUR OWN GALLERY

The great advantage of using ClipArt is that all of the images are stored in a convenient place and are also categorized – making life even easier. PowerPoint 2000 also allows you to modify and expand the ClipArt gallery by adding any of your own images, and setting up your own categories to group them.

1 OPEN THE CLIPART DIALOG BOX

● Choose **Picture** from the **Insert** menu and select **Clip Art** from the submenu.

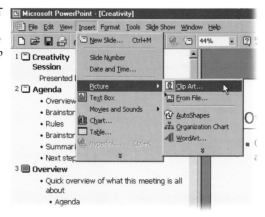

2 CREATING A NEW CATEGORY

● The **Insert ClipArt** dialog box opens. Click on the **New Category** button. The **New Category** dialog box opens. Type in the name for your new category and click on **OK**. The new category – **Dogs** – appears in the main window.

*The **New Category** button* ●

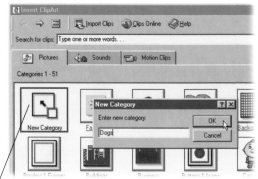

3 ADDING PICTURES

● To add pictures to your new category, single-click to highlight the icon. The **Insert ClipArt** window opens. Click on the **Import Clips** button at the top of the window.

● The **Add clip to Clip Gallery** dialog box opens. You can specify any (or all) of the pictures you want to include. Before initiating the command, take a quick look at the options at the bottom of the window – the top two options allow you either to make copies of the pictures to go into the gallery or simply move the existing picture. Click on the image to be added, and then click on **Import**.

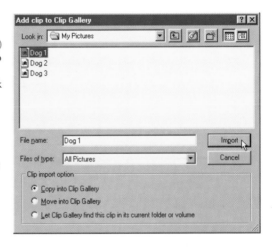

● The **Clip Properties** dialog box opens. Enter a description of the clip. This description will appear in a ScreenTip when you hover over the thumbnail of the clip when it finally appears in the ClipArt gallery.

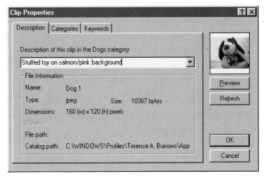

4 DEFINING CATEGORIES

● You can choose in which categories the new clip will appear in the ClipArt gallery. Click on the **Categories** tab in the **Clip Properties** dialog box.

● As the **Dogs** category was selected earlier, you will see that this category is checked when you scroll down the list.

● Click in the check box next to any of the categories in which you want the clip to be available. You are not duplicating the clip each time – you are attaching the clip's details to each category that you choose.

● Click on **OK** when you have made your selections.

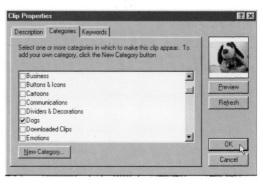

● If you return to the front page of the gallery, you can see that your new category also uses the first-loaded image as its icon.

SPECIAL ILLUSTRATION METHODS

We'll end this section on advanced design with a look at some of the more interesting features of the Drawing toolbar. There are a number of color, shape, and text options on this toolbar, but here we deal with lines and effects.

1 OPEN THE DRAW-ING TOOLBAR

● To open the Drawing toolbar, select **Toolbars** from the **View** menu, and click on **Drawing**.

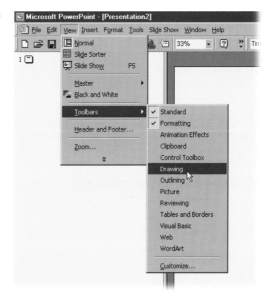

2 USING THE LINE TOOL

● Click on the **AutoShapes** button on the Drawing toolbar and select **Lines** from the pop-up menu. A submenu of tools appears. Click on the **Line** tool.

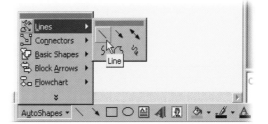

● The mouse pointer becomes a crosshair cursor. Hold down the left mouse button when the cursor is at the start position, drag the mouse to draw the line and release the mouse button at the end position of the line.

● The line appears with a handle at either end. You can alter the position of the line by clicking on one of the handles, holding down the mouse button and dragging the handle to its new location where you can release the mouse button.

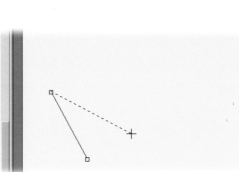

3 USING THE CURVE TOOL

● The lower three options on the **Lines** menu are for creating curved or freehand lines. Click on the **Curve** tool.

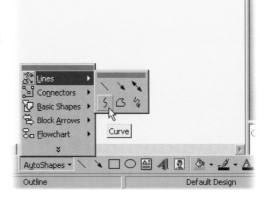

● Move the pointer to the start position of the line. Click on the mouse button (don't hold down the mouse button this time). Drag the mouse to draw the line and click once at each point where you want the line to curve. Repeat for as many curves as you wish to create. After your final curve, double-click to end.

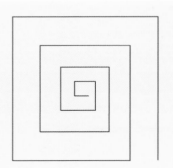

4 DRAWING FREEFORMS

● The **Freeform** tool can be used to create a wide variety of shapes.
● Click on the **Freeform** tool in the **Lines** options.

● The mouse cursor becomes a crosshair icon. To draw shapes that consist of straight lines, click once when the cross hair is positioned where the shape is to begin and drag the mouse to create the first straight line. Click once to change the direction of the line and drag the mouse in the new direction.
● To end the drawing, either double-click or press the Esc key.

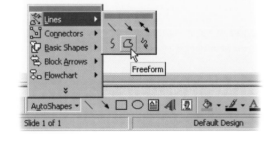

5 SHADOWS AND 3-D

● You can add shadow and 3-D effects to any Drawing object. This hexagon was drawn by going to the **AutoShapes** menu 📄, selecting **Basic Shapes**, clicking on the **Hexagon** icon, and then clicking and dragging on the slide. The color is added by clicking on the **Fill** tool on the Drawing toolbar 📄 and selecting the color.

● Select the hexagon and click on the **Shadow** tool to display the pop-up menu.
● Select a shadow style by clicking on it.

The Shadow tool ●

● The hexagon now has a shadow behind it, which suggests that it is being lit from the front.

📄 **㊷ AutoShapes**
11 menu

📄 **㊿ Fill**
11 Color

● The 3-D effects work in much the same way. Select the object and click on the **3-D** tool to display the pop-up menu and select a 3-D effect.

The 3-D tool ●

● The 3-D effect is now applied to the hexagon.

TILTING AN IMAGE

Although PowerPoint 2000 gives you a wide variety of 3-D effects, you may find that you want to alter the options available. One way of doing this is by using the tilt feature, which allows you to freely rotate the object. To do this, select the object you wish to rotate, and then click on the **3-D** tool on

●*Tilt down* ●*Tilt right*

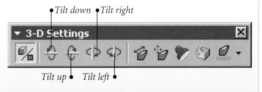

Tilt up ● *Tilt left* ●

the **Drawing** toolbar to select it. Click on **3-D Settings** at the foot of the pop-up menu and the **3-D Settings** toolbar opens.

Depending on which way you want to tilt the object, click either on the **Tilt down, Tilt up, Tilt left,** or **Tilt right** tools.

ADDING SOUND

No presentation can hope to succeed if it is delivered in silence.
The usual sound accompaniment is a script, which can be
recorded, but adding music as well is easy and effective.

USING SOUND CLIPS

A high-quality slide presentation consisting of text, ClipArt, and other images such as graphs can be extremely effective. However, you can give your presentations a whole new dimension with the use of sound. You can do this in several different ways: you can use sound clips provided with PowerPoint, music files and other sounds downloaded from the internet, and tracks from CDs.

HARDWARE AND SOUND CLIPS

● To make the most of sound files, you need to make sure that you first have the right hardware connected. The basic requirement for listening to sounds or recording your own audio is a sound card, and a CD-ROM drive if you want to access a CD.
● You don't actually have to record any new sound at all if you don't want to – PowerPoint 2000 comes equipped with its own gallery of sound clips.

SOUND FILES

You can use two different types of sound file in conjunction with PowerPoint 2000. The WAV music file format is the standard way of recording audio on a PC. These particular files are recognizable from their .wav suffix. PowerPoint 2000 can also work with MIDI files. MIDI is a language that allows suitably equipped musical instruments and computers to communicate with one another. For most PC owners, the easiest way to use MIDI is to access sounds that are loaded onto your computer's sound card. We won't discuss the complexities of MIDI here – if you want to discover more, you can refer to *Playing Music On Your PC* title in this *DK Essential Computers* series.

1 THE INSERT SOUND OPTION

● Begin by displaying the slide to which you want to add a sound clip.
● Select **Movies and Sounds** in the **Insert** menu, and from the submenu, select **Sound from Gallery**.

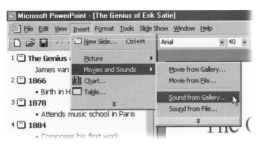

2 CHOOSING A SOUND

● The **Insert Sound** dialog box opens.
● Select a sound category by clicking on one of the icons – in this case, **Music**.

● The contents of the window are replaced by a set of icons. Each one of these represents a pre-recorded sound.
● Single-click on any icon to display a pop-up toolbar with further options.
● To audition the sound, click on the **Play clip** button.

The Play clip button ●

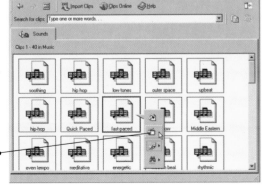

● The play sound panel opens and the sound plays automatically – the sound cursor moves along the panel and a digital display shows the elapsed time.

● You can stop or pause the sound by clicking on the appropriate buttons at the bottom left-hand corner of the window. When the sound finishes, the window automatically closes.

● *Pause button*   ● *Stop button*

QUICK SEARCHES FOR CLIPS

You may have noticed the text box marked **Search for clips** in the **Insert Sound** window. This feature allows you to locate sound clips if you know them by name. If you overtype the text **Type one or more words** with the sound clip's name, PowerPoint 2000 finds it for you.

3 INSERTING THE SOUND

● To add the sound to your slide, click on the icon and click on the **Insert clip** button on the toolbar.

● Close the **Insert Sound** dialog box. A confirmation panel appears asking if you want the sound to play automatically when the slide is shown. If you click on **Yes**, this will happen. If you click on **No**, a sound icon appears on the slide, but you have to click on the icon during the slide show to play the sound. In this example, **Yes** is selected.

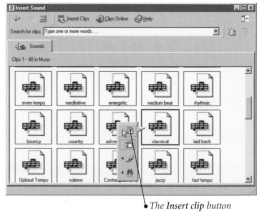

● *The Insert clip button*

● The sound icon is automatically positioned in the center of the slide. To reposition the icon anywhere within the slide, click on it, hold down the mouse button, drag the icon to the new location, and release the mouse button.

The sound icon ●

● If you click the **Slide Show** button to run the presentation, and you selected the automatic play option earlier, you will hear the sound when the slide is displayed during a presentation.

*The **Slide Show** button* ●

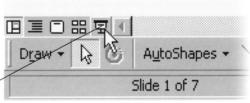

4 INSERTING OTHER SOUNDS

● You are not restricted to using only the sounds that you find in the sound clip gallery. You can also access any other sound files that you have on your hard disk. These may be examples you've recorded for yourself or downloaded from the internet (where you can find a great deal of free material).

● Select the slide to which you wish to attach the sound.

● Select **Movies and Sounds** in the **Insert** menu and select **Sound from File** from the submenu.

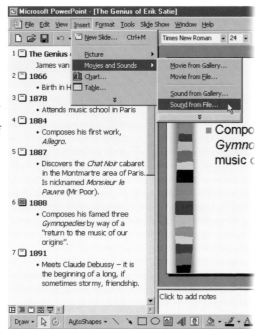

● The **Insert Sound** window opens. Navigate through the folder hierarchy until you find the sound file that you are looking for. Click on **OK**.

● You can determine when the sound plays, and the position of the sound icon on the slide, by using the same methods that were used with sounds from the sound clip gallery ⌐.

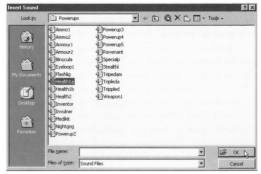

5 PLAYING SOUNDS FROM A CD

● You can also integrate sounds from any audio CD, providing you have a CD-ROM drive installed on your computer. This can be particularly useful for playing appropriate background music without having to go through the process of copying and converting the audio track to a sound file on your hard disk.

● Select the slide to which the sound is to be attached.
● Select **Movies and Sounds** in the **Insert** menu, and from the submenu choose **Play CD Audio Track**. (Click on the down-pointing double arrow at the foot of the menu if this option is not visible.)
● The **Movie and Sound Options** dialog box opens. In the **Play CD audio track** section, you can select the start and end points of the music to be played. In each case, you must specify the **Track** number and the time in minutes and seconds **At** which the audio must start and finish.
● If you want to create a continuous sound, click in the **Loop until stopped** check box – as soon as the sound gets to the end point it will start again from the beginning until stopped manually.
● Click on **OK** once you have made your selections.

● The sound icon again appears in the center of the slide and can be dragged into a more appropriate location.

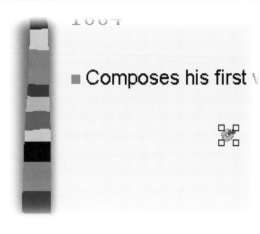

● Notice that this icon is distinct from the icon of the straightforward sound files that you have previously loaded.

SAVING SPACE

The next few pages deal with adding your own audio narration to a PowerPoint 2000 presentation. Although this is a highly organized way of keeping all the slide and sound information together, sound files take up a lot of disk space. If you have recording facilities, for example, a CD-R recorder on which you can make your own CDs, it may be more efficient to record the narratives for each slide onto a different track of a CD. You can then play them back as shown above.

RECORDING YOUR OWN NARRATION

It is possible to stand alongside your presentation and read out a script for each slide to the audience. However, in some cases it may be more appropriate to record your narration in advance by using PowerPoint 2000's sound recording facility. The two hardware requirements are a sound card and a microphone. These days it is not unusual to find these items bundled together in an all-in-one package.

There are two ways in which you can record a narration in PowerPoint 2000. You can do it one slide at a time, or record the whole presentation in one pass.

The most important place to begin is with your script. Make sure that you have a detailed plan for what you want to say for each slide. Unless you possess a rare talent, ad-libbing a commentary will sound awkward and unprofessional.

1 RECORDING THE SHOW

● If you wish, you can record the entire script for your presentation in one pass, viewing all the slides while you record.

● Go to the **Slide Show** menu and select **Record Narration**.

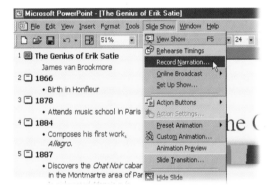

● The **Record Narration** dialog box opens. To check that your microphone is connected and that the record level is correctly set, click on the **Set Microphone Level** button.

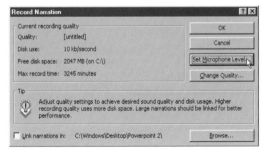

● The **Microphone Check** dialog box opens. If the signal is too quiet, it won't be audible; if it is too loud, the sound will distort – you can see this if the meter extends into the red region. Click on **OK**.

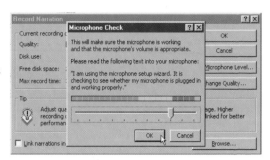

● You can adjust the sound quality by clicking on the **Change Quality** button in the **Record Narration** dialog box.

● The **Sound Selection** dialog box opens, allowing you to set the format of the file you are about to record. For the best quality sound, choose **CD Quality** from the **Name** list, and **44,100 Hz, 16 Bit Stereo** from the **Attributes** list. Don't forget, though, that the higher quality the sound, the more hard disk space you use. Click on **OK** to return to the **Record Narration** dialog box.

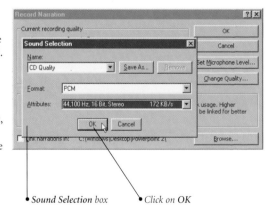

• *Sound Selection box*   • *Click on OK*

2 RECORDING SINGLE SLIDES

● Begin by selecting the slide that is to be the subject of the recording. Select **Movies and Sounds** from the **Insert** menu. From the submenu, choose **Record Sound**.

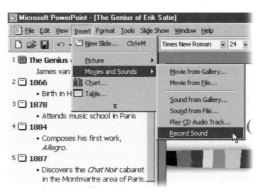

● The **Record Sound** dialog box opens. Enter a name for the sound file. Remember, this sound is only related to this particular slide, and it's useful to refer to the slide in the file name.

● To start recording your narration, click on the **Record** button. When you have finished, click on the **Stop** button. You can listen to what you have recorded by clicking on the **Play** button.

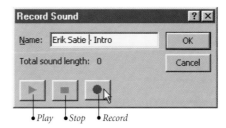

● *Play* ● *Stop* ● *Record*

SOUND QUALITY

The sound you record is stored digitally, and has the potential to reproduce CD-quality sound. However, if the original sound quality is poor as a result of using inferior equipment, the output quality will also be poor. The key lies in the quality of the microphone that is used. Microphones vary widely in price with the most sensitive valve microphones costing thousands of dollars. Unfortunately, the microphones that are built into PCs are often inferior and prevent your computer from delivering the sound quality it is capable of. So, to produce polished presentations, you should try to use a high-quality microphone.

MACROS AND TOOLBARS

This final section deals with tips about using the program more efficiently. For example, macros can automate tasks, and other features can be customized according to your needs.

DEALING WITH MACROS

A macro is a set of commands that automatically performs predetermined routine tasks without any further intervention. PowerPoint 2000's macros are created using a language called Visual Basic for Applications (VBA), which is installed with the program. This is a cut-down version of the widely used Visual Basic programming language. However, you don't need to be a computer programmer in order to produce impressive results using PowerPoint 2000. The simplest form of macro is one that

lets you record a series of keystrokes. These can then be repeated by issuing a single command whenever they are required. This feature can be useful in many different circumstances, such as adding multiple new slides to a presentation. In the example that follows, all that exists in the presentation is the summary slide. We'll now set up a macro for inserting new slides when required, which contain the company name and logo (in the form an image in a file) automatically placed in position.

1 RECORDING A MACRO

● Choose **Macro** from the **Tools** menu. From the submenu, select **Record New Macro**. (Click on the down-pointing double arrow at the foot of the menu if this option is not visible.)

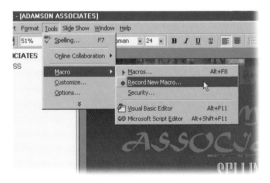

● The **Record Macro** dialog box opens. Here you can enter a name for the macro, specify the folder in which it is to be stored, and add descriptive text to outline what the macro does, or its origins. Notice that the macro name has underscore characters between each word; this is because macro names cannot contain spaces.

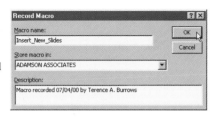

● Click on **OK** to start the macro – from this point onward, all keystrokes are recorded. The **Stop Recording** toolbar appears on the screen.

*The **Stop Recording** toolbar ●*

● Carry out the steps to create a new slide that contains a company name and logo.

● This is only an exercise, so you can afford to use whatever formatting you choose, simply in order to experiment.

● When you have finished recording the keystrokes, click on the Stop button in the **Stop Recording** toolbar.

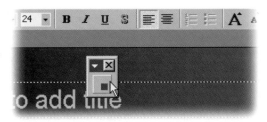

2 REPLAYING YOUR MACRO

● Stopping the macro ends the recording of the keystrokes and saves the macro. By replaying the macro you've just created and stored, all the keystrokes that you carried out between starting and ending the recording are replayed automatically.

● Choose **Macro** from the **Tools** menu, and from the submenu select **Macros**.

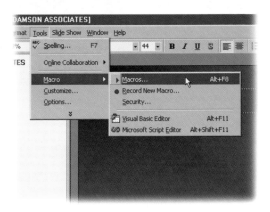

● The **Macro** window opens. Select the macro you want to use from the list, and click on **Run**.

● In barely an instant, a
new slide is created with
the correct formatting, text,
and image in place.
● In this particular case, it
clearly would have been
simpler to use the **Copy**
and **Paste** commands to
duplicate the slide
template. However, this was
a deliberately simple
example to show how
simple macros are to create
and run. A macro can
contain thousands of
keystrokes.

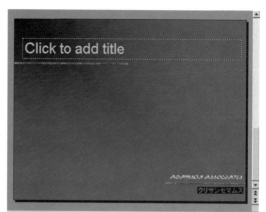

3 DELETING MACROS

● Once you become
familiar with how to create
and use macros, and
discover how easy they are
to write, you will find that
macros accumulate on your
hard disk, and you will
forget what the old ones
did. Deleting old macros is
good practice.

● To get rid of old or
unwanted macros, begin by
following the instructions
for replaying a macro from
the **Tools** menu ⬚.

● This time, when you
get to the **Macro** window,
choose your macro and
then click on the **Delete**
button.

⬚ 60 Replaying your macro

CUSTOMIZING TOOLBARS

Like the most powerful modern software, PowerPoint 2000 is extremely flexible and offers many different possible approaches to any one function. Furthermore, the wealth of features is designed to cater to the needs of a wide variety of different users, which means that many of us will only use a small proportion the available commands. The result is that some of the toolbar options will only have a limited use for many people. Once again, PowerPoint 2000 presents a solution – why not create custom-made toolbars geared toward your own needs?

1 CREATING A NEW TOOLBAR

● From the **Tools** menu choose **Customize**.

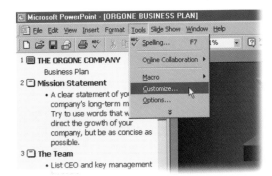

● The **Customize** window opens. Click on the **Toolbars** tab if it is not already displayed, and then click on the **New** button.

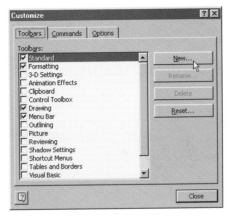

2 CHOOSING A NAME

● The **New Toolbar** dialog box appears. Type in a unique name for your toolbar and click on **OK**.

● You'll see that the new toolbar name is displayed in the **Toolbars** list. You'll also see the new toolbar floating to the left of the **Customize** window.

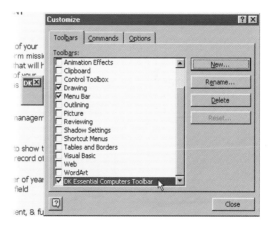

3 POSITIONING THE TOOLBAR

● Double-click on the title bar of the new, small toolbar, and it is repositioned at the top of the screen below the other active toolbars. As you haven't yet specified any content, it is currently empty.

The newly created, empty toolbar

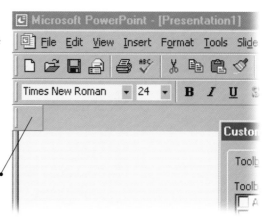

ADDING TO THE TOOLBAR

The next set of examples shows you how you can add commands to the new toolbar that you just created. It is also possible to add to or edit existing toolbars at the top of the screen by using the same techniques.

1 OPENING THE COMMANDS TAB

● In the **Customize** window click on the **Commands** tab. (If you closed the window after the previous exercise, reopen it by choosing **Customize** from the **Tools** menu.)

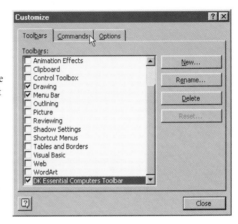

2 SELECTING A CATEGORY

● The **Commands** tab contains a list of categories on the left and a list of commands on the right. As the commands relate directly to the categories, choosing a different category will create a different selection of command options.

● In this example, click on the **Animation Effects** category.

3 SELECTING A COMMAND

● Select the **Camera** command from the list on the right. If you want to check what it does, click on **Description**.

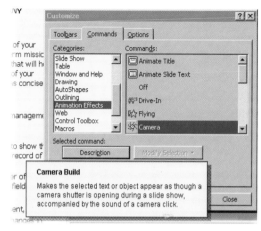

Camera Build

Makes the selected text or object appear as though a camera shutter is opening during a slide show, accompanied by the sound of a camera click.

● Drag the command and release the icon at the beginning of the toolbar. A black I-beam will appear when you are at the correct position.

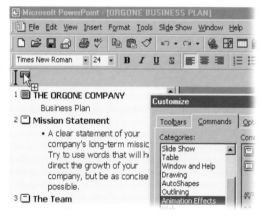

● When you release the mouse button, the command's icon will be seen on the toolbar.

New command on the toolbar ●

● You can repeat steps 2 and 3, and add as many other tools as you wish. Close the **Customize** window when you have finished.

● *The new toolbar*

DELETING TOOLBAR COMMANDS

You can easily remove commands from your new toolbar (or any other toolbar, for that matter). To do this, you must

again use the **Customize** window, but this time we will drag from the toolbar the commands that are no longer required.

1 OPENING THE CUSTOMIZE BOX

● In the **View** menu, select **Toolbars**. From the submenu, click on **Customize**.

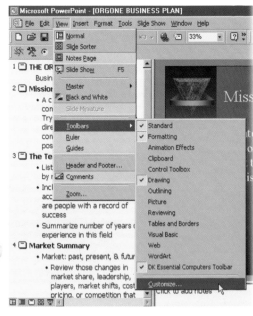

2 REMOVING FROM THE TOOLBAR

● The **Customize** window opens. Move to the toolbar and drag the command button that you want to delete away from the toolbar. When the mouse pointer's icon changes so that it has a small "x" in the bottom right-hand corner, release the button.

Command to be removed ●

Command being dragged from toolbar ●

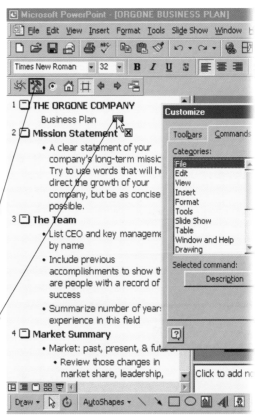

● The command has now been deleted from the toolbar.

The existing buttons move along to fill the vacated space ●

ADDING A MACRO TO THE TOOLBAR

You have already seen how macros can be used to save time when performing repetitive tasks. You can make macros even more flexible and easier to use by adding them to your own toolbars, just like any other commands.

1 SELECTING THE MACRO

● Begin by opening the **Customize** window by selecting **Toolbars** from the **View** menu and clicking on **Customize** in the submenu.

● In the **Customize** window, click on the **Commands** tab to bring it to the front. From the **Categories** list, choose **Macros**. This lists the macros that have been created for this presentation.

● Highlight the macro that you want to use and drag it onto the toolbar.

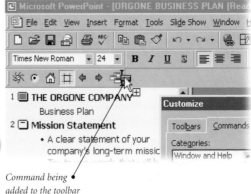

Command being added to the toolbar

2 CHANGING TO AN ICON

● As you can see, a button marked **Insert_Slides** has been placed on the toolbar. To make better use of space, you can allocate an icon to the command. With the button still highlighted (it should have a black frame around the outside of the button), click on **Modify Selection**. From the pop-up list, choose **Default Style**. This removes the text on the toolbar.

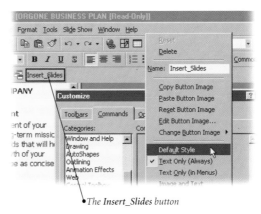

The Insert_Slides button

● With the icon still highlighted, click again on **Modify Selection**. This time choose **Change Button Image** from the pop-up menu. This opens up a submenu of button icons. Click on the one that you want to appear on the toolbar. Click on **Close** to shut the **Customize** window.

● The icon now appears on the toolbar.

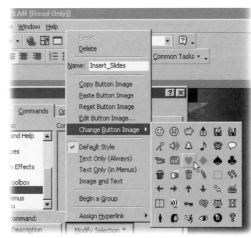

New image on toolbar

GLOSSARY

ANIMATION
Creation of moving elements within a presentation.

AUTOCONTENT WIZARD
A set of interactive instructions allowing for the selection of a series of existing presentations that can be modified for personal use.

BLANK PRESENTATION
Creating a new presentation starting with no existing design elements in place. An alternative to a pre-designed AutoContent presentation.

BULLET
Icon that appears at the start of each point in a list. PowerPoint offers a range of bullet styles.

COLLAPSING
Hiding bulleted points so that only the heading is visible.

DATASHEET
A spreadsheet-style window containing figures for use in charts and graphs. Changing the data in the sheet produces changes in the visual display.

DEMOTING
Moving bulleted items toward the bottom of the list.

DESIGN TEMPLATE
A professionally designed presentation outline that can be used as a basis for new presentations.

DRAWING TOOLBAR
Set of icons for the creation of graphic images in presentation slides.

EXPANDING
Making bulleted points visible beneath a heading. The opposite of collapsing.

FONT
The typeface in which text appears on the screen and when printed out.

FORMATTING TOOLBAR
Set of icons for altering the design of text in a presentation, such as font, type style and size, alignment and justification, and number format.

HANDOUT
Printed version of slide presentation given to the audience to accompany a presentation.

MICROSOFT GRAPH 2000
Software that can be installed with PowerPoint 2000 for the creation of charts and graphs.

NAME
Title given to a presentation before saving it on the hard drive of a PC.

NORMAL VIEW
Screen view in which text and visual elements are given equal proportions of the screen.

OBJECT
Any element of a slide, such as text, image, or sound.

ORGANIZATION CHART
A hierarchical box chart often used to illustrate the chain of command within a corporation.

OUTLINE VIEW
Screen view in which the text is the main element.

PRESENTATION
A series of linked single-screen slides viewed in sequence.

PROMOTING
Moving bulleted items toward the top of the list.

RESIZING
Dragging the edges of an object to alter its size.

SAVE
Command used to store a presentation on a PC's hard drive.

SLIDE
Single screen from a presentation.

SLIDE SHOW
Screen view in which the presentation can be viewed as a whole.

SLIDE SORTER
Screen view in which all of the slides in a presentation can be viewed in thumbnail form.

SLIDE VIEW
Screen view in which the slide design can be seen.

STANDARD TOOLBAR
A series of icons that contains shortcuts for basic functions such as opening new files or copying, cutting, and pasting objects.

WORDART
Function of the Drawing Toolbar that allows for the creation of stylized headline text in a variety of colors and shapes.

INDEX

ACKNOWLEDGMENTS

PUBLISHER'S ACKNOWLEDGMENTS
Dorling Kindersley would like to thank the following:
Paul Mattock of APM, Brighton, for commissioned photography.
Microsoft Corporation for permission to reproduce screens
from within Microsoft® PowerPoint® 2000.

Every effort has been made to trace the copyright holders.
The publisher apologizes for any unintentional omissions and would be pleased,
in such cases, to place an acknowledgment in future editions of this book.

Microsoft is a registered trademark of Microsoft Corporation
in the United States and/or other countries.